HOUGHTON MIFFLIN

Community Ties

Senior Authors

J. David Cooper
John J. Pikulski

Authors

Kathryn H. Au
Margarita Calderón
Jacqueline C. Comas
Marjorie Y. Lipson
J. Sabrina Mims
Susan E. Page
Sheila W. Valencia
MaryEllen Vogt

Consultants

Dolores Malcolm
Tina Saldivar
Shane Templeton

Acknowledgments appear on page Acknowledgments 1 at the back of this book.

1999 Impression

Printed in the U.S.A.   ISBN: 0-395-79515-X   89-WC-03 02 01 00 99

INVITATIONS TO LITERACY

Houghton Mifflin Company • Boston

Atlanta • Dallas • Geneva, Illinois • Palo Alto • Princeton

Community Ties

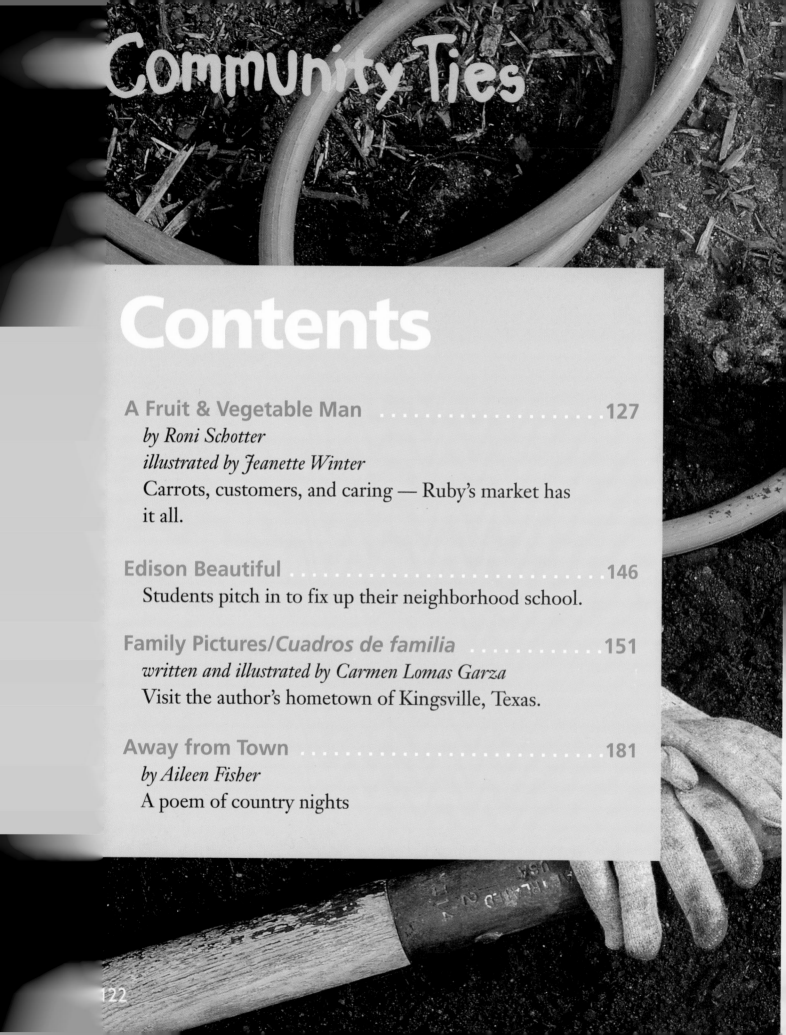

Community Ties

Contents

A Fruit & Vegetable Man 127
by Roni Schotter
illustrated by Jeanette Winter
Carrots, customers, and caring — Ruby's market has it all.

Edison Beautiful 146
Students pitch in to fix up their neighborhood school.

Family Pictures/*Cuadros de familia* 151
written and illustrated by Carmen Lomas Garza
Visit the author's hometown of Kingsville, Texas.

Away from Town 181
by Aileen Fisher
A poem of country nights

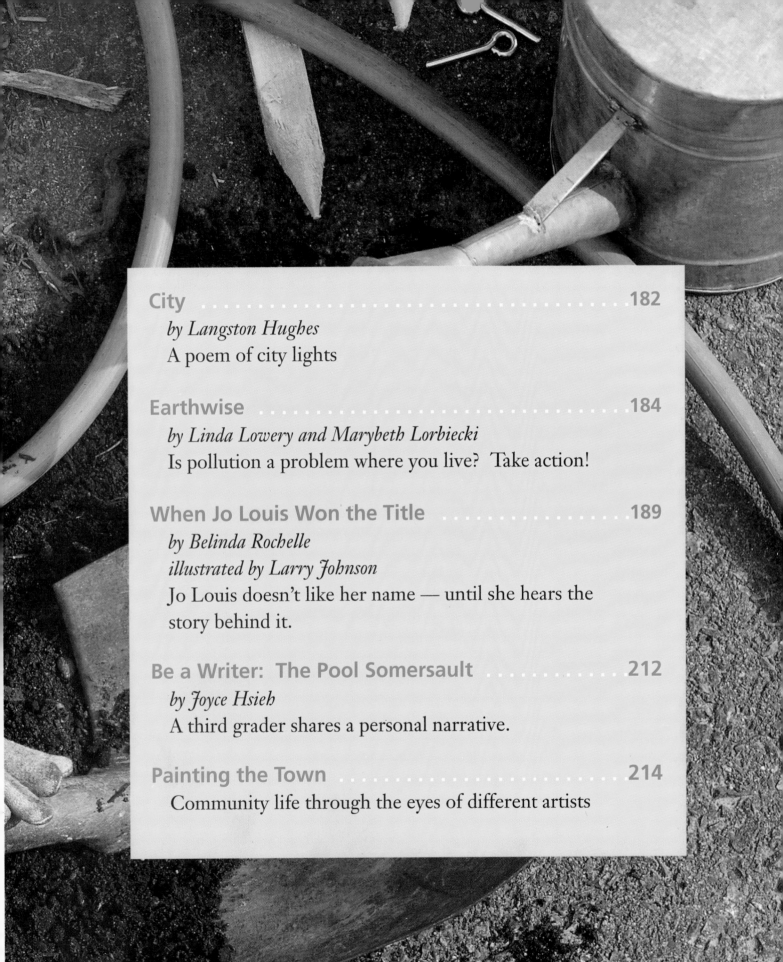

City 182
  by Langston Hughes
  A poem of city lights

Earthwise 184
  by Linda Lowery and Marybeth Lorbiecki
  Is pollution a problem where you live? Take action!

When Jo Louis Won the Title 189
  by Belinda Rochelle
  illustrated by Larry Johnson
  Jo Louis doesn't like her name — until she hears the
  story behind it.

Be a Writer: The Pool Somersault 212
  by Joyce Hsieh
  A third grader shares a personal narrative.

Painting the Town 214
  Community life through the eyes of different artists

Community Ties

Read On Your Own

My Buddy
by Audrey Osofsky

Buddy is no ordinary Golden Retriever — he's a working dog who makes life easier for his master.

In the same book . . .
An article about a young dog trainer, a matching game to test your dog knowledge, and more

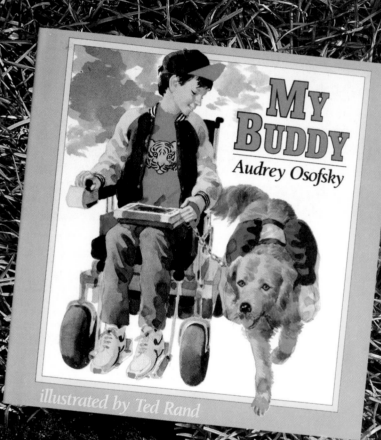

MY BUDDY
Audrey Osofsky

illustrated by Ted Rand

Cam Jansen and the Mystery of the Babe Ruth Baseball

by David A. Adler

Cam Jansen covers all the bases in her search for a stolen baseball signed by the Babe.

In the same book . . .
More about baseball, including statistics and card-collecting tips

Stories from Around Town

Tar Beach
by Faith Ringgold
Dreams come true on a magical summer night in New York City.

Pearl Moscowitz's Last Stand
by Arthur Levine
Mrs. Moscowitz takes on City Hall to save the gingko trees in her neighborhood.

Vejigante Masquerader
by Lulu Delacre
Will Ramón finish his costume in time for the annual carnival?

Eskimo Boy: Life in an Inupiaq Eskimo Village
by Russ Kendall
An Eskimo boy takes you on a tour of his Alaskan village.

Fly Away Home
by Eve Bunting
Andrew and his father hope for a real home and a brighter future.

About the Author

Roni Schotter doesn't have to look far for story ideas. When she lived in New York City, she saw many fruit and vegetable stands in the streets. The fruits and vegetables were as colorful to look at as they were good to eat. That's what inspired her to write *A Fruit & Vegetable Man*.

About the Illustrator

Jeanette Winter likes to draw. Sometimes she likes to write. And sometimes she likes to do both, as she did in the book *Follow the Drinking Gourd*. In her spare time, when she's not drawing or writing, Winter enjoys taking photographs.

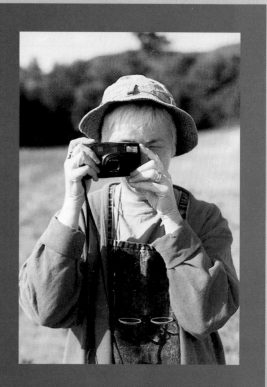

•A•
FRUIT & VEGETABLE
MAN

by Roni Schotter
Pictures by Jeanette Winter

Ruby Rubenstein was a fruit and vegetable man. His motto was "I take care." Six mornings a week, long before the sun was up, Ruby was.

"*Is it time*, Ruby?" his wife Trudy always asked from deep under the covers.

"It's time," Ruby always answered. Then he'd jump out of bed, touch his knees, then his toes, and hurry uptown to market to choose the ripest fruit and vegetables for his store.

For nearly fifty years it had been so — ever since he and Trudy first sailed across the ocean to make a new life together.

Every morning before school, Sun Ho and his sister, Young Mee, who with their family, had just flown across the sky to make a new life together, came to watch Ruby work his magic.

"Yo-ho, Mr. Ruby!" Sun Ho would call out. "Show me!"

And nodding to Sun Ho, Ruby would pile apples, tangerines, and pears in perfect pyramids, arrange grapes in diamonds, insert a head of lettuce as accent, then tuck in a bunch of broccoli or a bit of watercress for trim.

It was like seeing a great artist at work. Sun Ho felt honored to be there. "Like a painting, Mr. Ruby!" he would say shyly.

Ruby always smiled, and his smile filled Sun Ho with happiness and, deep inside, a strange feeling that was like wishing. Sun Ho watched as Ruby juggled cantaloupes, then cut them into wedges and packed them neatly in plastic. Inside Sun Ho, the feeling that was like wishing grew stronger.

GRANNY SMITH
SPECIAL
3/1.<u>00</u>

"He's an artist, all right," Old Ella from up the block always said, pocketing an apple and a handful of prunes.

Ruby didn't mind. He'd just wink and utter one wonderful word: "Taste!" Then he'd offer whatever he had on special that day to Sun Ho, his sister, and anyone who wanted.

"What would we *do* without Ruby?" Mary Morrissey asked the crowd one gray afternoon. The people of Delano Street sighed and shook their heads at such a terrible thought.

"Mr. Ruby," Sun Ho said, "he's one of a kind."

Yes, everyone on Delano Street appreciated Ruby. But Ruby was getting old. Lately, when he got up to

touch his knees and his toes, there was a stiffness Ruby pretended he didn't feel and a creaking Trudy pretended she didn't hear. And sometimes, though Ruby never would admit it, there was a wish that he could stay a little longer in bed with Trudy.

"Ruby," Trudy said to him one morning from under the covers. "Long ago you and I made a promise. We said if ever we got old, we'd sell the business and go to live in the mountains. *Is it time, Ruby?*"

"NO!!" Ruby thundered. And he leapt out of bed, did *twice* his usual number of exercises, and ran off to market.

As if to prove he was as young as ever, he worked especially hard at the store that day and made some of his most beautiful designs.

That afternoon, Sun Ho came by as Ruby was arranging potatoes in his own special way. Sun Ho watched as Ruby whirled them in the air and tossed them with such skill that they landed perfectly, one next to the other in a neat row.

"Yo-ho, Mr. Ruby!" Sun Ho said, filled with admiration. "Teach me?"

Proudly, Ruby grabbed an Idaho and two russets and taught Sun Ho how to juggle. Next he taught him how to pile grapefruits to keep them from falling. By the time Sun Ho's parents stopped by, Ruby had even taught Sun Ho how to work the register. Then he sat Sun Ho down and told him how, early every morning, he went to market to choose his fruit and vegetables.

"Take me!" Sun Ho pleaded, the feeling that was like wishing so big now he felt he might burst. "Please?"

Ruby thought only for a moment. Then he spoke. "My pleasure," he announced.

So early the next day, while Venus still sparkled in the dark morning sky, Ruby took Sun Ho to market. Sun Ho

had an excellent nose, and together he and Ruby sniffed
out the most fragrant fruit and sampled the choicest
chicory. Then Ruby showed Sun Ho how he talked and
teased and argued his way to the best prices.

All the rest of that long day, Sun Ho felt special. And Ruby? He felt, well . . . tired. Whenever Trudy was busy with a customer, Ruby leaned over and pretended to tie his shoe, but what he did, really, was *yawn*. By afternoon, Ruby was running out of the store every few minutes. "The fruit!" he'd yell to Trudy. "Got to fix the fruit!" he'd say, but once outside, what he did, really, was *sneeze*.

"To your health, Mr. Ruby," Sun Ho whispered, sneaking him a handkerchief.

"Thank you, Mr. Sun Ho," Ruby said, quietly blowing his nose.

That evening it began to snow on Delano Street. It snowed all night, and by morning the street was cold and white, the color of fresh cauliflower.

For the first time in many years, Ruby woke up feeling sick. His face was red, his forehead hot. "No work today," Trudy said. "Ruby's Fruit and Vegetable is closed until further notice." What would the people of Delano Street do without him? Ruby wondered. But he was too sick to care.

When Sun Ho arrived at the store that day and saw that it was closed, he was worried. Where was Ruby?

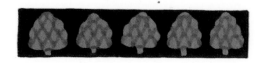

Upstairs in his bed, Ruby dozed, dreaming of spring and fresh apricots. Once, when he opened his eyes, Sun Ho was standing next to him . . . or was he?

"No worries," Sun Ho seemed to say. "I take care." Then as strangely as he had appeared, Sun Ho disappeared. Was Ruby dreaming?

For the next three days, for the first time in his life, Ruby was too sick to think or worry about his store. He

stayed deep under the covers, enjoying Trudy's loving
care, and more than that, her barley soup. On the
morning of the fourth day, he felt well enough to worry.
On the morning of the fifth day, a Saturday, there was no
stopping him. "My store!" he shouted. Leaning on
Trudy's arm, he put on his clothes. Then he rushed off to
reopen.

What a surprise when he arrived! The store was open. In fact, it looked as if it had never been shut. The peppers were in pyramids, the dates in diamonds, the winter tomatoes in triangles. Sun Ho's father was helping Old Ella to a pound of carrots. Sun Ho's mother was at the register. Young Mee was polishing pears. And, in the center of it all, Sun Ho stood smiling, offering customers a taste of something new — bean sprouts!

When they saw Ruby, everyone cheered. Ruby bowed with pleasure.

"I took care, Mr. Ruby!" Sun Ho called out proudly.

"I see," Ruby answered. "You're a fruit and vegetable man, Sun Ho, like me."

Sun Ho's face turned the color of Ruby's radishes. The feeling that was like wishing was gone now. In its place was a different feeling: pride.

"*Is it time*, Ruby?" Trudy whispered.

Ruby sighed. He thought about how much he liked Sun Ho and his family and how carefully they had kept his store. He thought about the stiffness and creaking in his knees. He thought about the mountains and about Trudy's loving care. More than that, he thought about her barley soup.

"It's time," he said finally.

Now Sun Ho is a fruit and vegetable man! Every morning, long before the sun is up, long before it's time for school, Sun Ho and his family are up, ready to hurry to market to choose the ripest fruit and vegetables for their store.

And Ruby? He's still a fruit and vegetable man . . . only now he and Trudy grow their own.

Ideas to Pick From

RESPONDING

Write a Letter

Dear Ruby, How Are You?

Write a letter to tell Ruby the news about his old store and neighborhood. What changes have been made? What things are still the same?

Finding Out About a Career

Learning on the Job

Sun Ho learned about running a store from an expert: Ruby. Find out about a job you'd like to have. Talk to someone who has that job, or read a book about it. Share what you learn.

EDISON BEAUTIFUL

photos by Fred Boyle

When the Thomas A. Edison Elementary School in Long Beach, California, needed sprucing up, more than 2,300 students, parents, teachers, and other volunteers got together with paintbrushes in hand.

Painting the flagpole in front of the school kept Jonny Keebler busy all day. "It was neat!" he said. "I was helping to work on a school to make it look better."

A total of 366 gallons of paint was used to give the school building a new look. On the wall surrounding the school, volunteers painted a mural designed by students. The mural is easy to spot from the off-ramp of the freeway.

People of all ages turned out for the two-day event, which was part of International Community Service Day. Local businesses donated most of the materials for the project, including eighty cypress trees and forty bushes.

148

After working hard, everyone was tired and ready to eat. Twenty-eight vanilla and chocolate sheet cakes were made into one enormous cake for the end-of-the-project celebration. Students at Edison Elementary couldn't wait to go to school on Monday!

Meet Carmen Lomas Garza

The pictures in this book are all painted from my memories of growing up in Kingsville, Texas, near the border with Mexico. From the time I was a young girl I always dreamed of becoming an artist. I practiced drawing every day; I studied art in school; and I finally did become an artist. My family has inspired and encouraged me for all these years. This is my book of family pictures.

Los cuadros de este libro los pinté de los recuerdos de mi niñez en Kingsville, Texas, cerca de la frontera con México. Desde que era pequeña, siempre soñé con ser artista. Dibujaba cada día; estudié arte en la escuela; y por fin, me hice artista. Mi familia me ha inspirado y alentado todos estos años. Éste es mi libro de cuadros de familia.

Family Pictures ◆ Cuadros de familia

CARMEN LOMAS GARZA

The Fair in Reynosa

My friends and I once went to a very big fair across the border in Reynosa, Mexico. The fair lasted a whole week. Artisans and entertainers came from all over Mexico. There were lots of booths with food and crafts. This is one little section where everybody is ordering and eating tacos.

I painted a father buying tacos and the rest of the family sitting down at the table. The little girl is the father's favorite and that's why she gets to tag along with him. I can always recognize little girls who are their fathers' favorites.

La Feria en Reynosa

Una vez, mis amigos y yo fuimos a una feria muy grande en Reynosa, México, al otro lado de la frontera. La feria duró una semana entera. Vinieron artesanos y artistas de todo México. Había muchos puestos que vendían comida y artesanías. Ésta es una pequeña parte de la feria donde todos están comprando tacos y comiéndoselos.

Pinté a un padre comprando tacos y al resto de la familia sentada a la mesa. La niñita pequeña es la preferida de su papá, y por eso es que él la permite acompañarlo. Aún hoy, siempre puedo reconocer cuando una niñita es la preferida de su papá.

Oranges

We were always going to my grandparents' house, so whatever they were involved in we would get involved in. In this picture my grandmother is hanging up the laundry. We told her that the oranges needed picking so she said, "Well, go ahead and pick some." Before she knew it, she had too many oranges to hold in her hands, so she made a basket out of her apron. That's my brother up in the tree, picking oranges. The rest of us are picking up the ones that he dropped on the ground.

Naranjas

Siempre íbamos a la casa de mis abuelos, así que cualquier cosa que estuvieran haciendo ellos, nosotros la hacíamos también. En este cuadro, mi abuela está colgando la ropa a secar. Nosotros le dijimos que las naranjas estaban listas para cosechar, y ella nos respondió: —Vayan pues, recójanlas. En un dos por tres, tenía demasiadas naranjas para sostenerlas en las manos, así que convirtió su delantal en canasta. Ése es mi hermano, en el árbol, recogiendo naranjas. El resto de nosotros estamos recogiendo las que él deja caer al suelo.

For Dinner

This is my grandparents' backyard. My grandmother is killing a chicken for dinner. My grandfather is in the chicken coop trying to catch another chicken. Later, my family will sit down to eat Sunday dinner — chicken soup.

That's me in the blue dress with my younger brother, Arturo. He was so surprised by the scene that he started to spill his snowcone. We had never seen anything like that before. I knew my grandparents had always raised chickens, but I never knew how the chickens got to be soup.

Para la cena

Éste es el patio de mis abuelos. Mi abuela está matando a una gallina para la cena. Mi abuelo está en el gallinero tratando de atrapar a otra gallina. Más tarde, mi familia se sentará a comer la cena del domingo: sopa de pollo.

Ésa soy yo, vestida de azul, con mi hermano menor, Arturo. Él estaba tan sorprendido por lo que veía que se le empezó a derramar su raspa. Nunca antes habíamos visto algo parecido. Yo sabía que mis abuelos criaban gallinas, pero no había sabido antes cómo era que las gallinas se convertían en sopa.

Birthday Party

That's me hitting the piñata at my sixth birthday party. It was also my brother's fourth birthday. My mother made a big birthday party for us and invited all kinds of friends, cousins and neighborhood kids.

You can't see the piñata when you're trying to hit it, because your eyes are covered with a handkerchief. My father is pulling the rope that makes the piñata go up and down. He will make sure that everybody has a chance to hit it at least once. Somebody will end up breaking it, and that's when all the candies will fall out and all the kids will run and try to grab them.

Cumpleaños

Ésa soy yo, pegándole a la piñata en la fiesta que me dieron cuando cumplí seis años. Era también el cumpleaños de mi hermano, que cumplía cuatro años. Mi madre nos dio una gran fiesta e invitó a muchos primos, vecinos y amigos.

No puedes ver la piñata cuando le estás dando con el palo, porque tienes los ojos cubiertos por un pañuelo. Mi padre está tirando de la cuerda que sube y baja la piñata. Él se encargará de que todos tengan por lo menos una oportunidad de pegarle a la piñata. Luego alguien acabará rompiéndola, y entonces todos los caramelos que tiene dentro caerán y todos los niños correrán a cogerlos.

159

Cakewalk

Cakewalk was a game to raise money to send Mexican Americans to the university. You paid 25 cents to stand on a number. When the music started, you walked around and around. When the music stopped, whatever number you happened to step on was your number. Then one of the ladies in the center would pick out a number from the can. If you were standing on the winning number, you would win a cake. That's my mother in the center of the circle in the pink and black dress. My father is serving punch. I'm the little girl in front of the store scribbling on the sidewalk with a twig.

Cakewalk

Cakewalk era un juego que se hacía para recaudar fondos para darles becas universitarias a jóvenes méxico-americanos. Se pagaba 25 centavos para poder pararse sobre un número. Cuando la música empezaba a tocar, todos empezaban a caminar en círculo. Cuando se terminaba la música, el número sobre el cual estabas parado era tu número. Entonces una de las señoras que estaba en el centro del círculo escogía un número de la lata. Si estabas parado sobre el número de la suerte, ganabas un pastel. Ésa es mi madre en el centro del círculo, vestida de rosado y negro. Mi papá está sirviendo ponche. Yo soy la niñita dibujando garabatos en la acera al frente de la tienda con una ramita.

Picking Nopal Cactus

In the early spring my grandfather would come and get us and we'd all go out into the woods to pick nopal cactus. My grandfather and my mother are slicing off the fresh, tender leaves of the nopal and putting them in boxes. My grandmother and my brother Arturo are pulling leaves from the mesquite tree to line the boxes. After we got home my grandfather would shave off all the needles from each leaf of cactus. Then my grandmother would parboil the leaves in hot water. The next morning she would cut them up and stir fry them with chili powder and eggs for breakfast.

Piscando nopalitos

Al comienzo de la primavera, mi abuelo nos venía a buscar y todos íbamos al bosque a piscar nopalitos. Mi abuelo y mi madre están cortando las pencas tiernas del nopal y metiéndolas en cajas. Mi abuela y mi hermano Arturo están recogiendo hojas de mesquite para forrar las cajas. Después que regresábamos a casa, mi abuelo le quitaba las espinas a cada penca del cactus. Luego mi abuela cocía las pencas en agua hirviente. A la mañana siguiente, las cortaba y las freía con chile y huevos para nuestro desayuno.

163

Hammerhead Shark

This picture is about the times my family went to Padre Island in the Gulf of Mexico to go swimming. Once when we got there, a fisherman had just caught a big hammerhead shark at the end of the pier. How he got the shark to the beach, I never found out. It was scary to see because it was big enough to swallow a little kid whole.

Tiburón martillo

Este cuadro trata de las veces que mi familia iba a nadar a la Isla del Padre en el Golfo de México. Una vez cuando llegamos, un pescador acababa de atrapar a un tiburón martillo al cabo del muelle. Cómo logró llevar al tiburón a la playa, nunca me enteré. Daba mucho miedo ver al tiburón, porque era tan grande que hubiera podido tragarse a un niño pequeño de un solo bocado.

Rabbit

My grandfather used to have a garden and also raise chickens and rabbits. In this painting, he is coming into the kitchen with a freshly prepared rabbit for dinner. My grandmother is making tortillas. That's my little brother, Arturo, sitting on the bench. He liked to watch my grandmother cook.   And that's my younger sister, Margie, playing jacks on the floor. I'm watching from my grandparents' bedroom which is next to the kitchen.

Conejo

Mi abuelo tenía un jardín, y también criaba pollos y conejos. En este cuadro, está entrando a la cocina con un conejo que acaba de preparar para la cena. Mi abuelita está preparando tortillas. Ése es mi hermano Arturo, sentado en la banca. Le gustaba mirar a mi abuela mientras cocinaba. Y ésa es mi hermana menor, Margie, jugando a los "jacks" en el suelo. Yo estoy mirando desde la recámara de mis abuelos, que está al lado de la cocina.

167

Joseph and Mary Seeking Shelter at the Inn

On each of the nine nights before Christmas we act out the story of Mary and Joseph seeking shelter at the inn. We call this custom "Las Posadas." A little girl and a little boy play Mary and Joseph and they are led by an angel.

Each night the travelers go to a different house. They knock on the door. When the door opens, they sing: "We are Mary and Joseph looking for shelter." At first the family inside refuses to let them in; then the travelers sing again. At last Joseph and Mary are let into the house. Then everybody comes in and we have a party.

Las Posadas

Cada una de las nueve noches antes de Nochebuena, representamos la historia de María y José buscando albergue en la posada. Esta costumbre se llama "Las Posadas". Una niñita y un niñito representan a María y José, y hay un ángel que les guía.

Cada noche, los caminantes van a una casa distinta. Tocan la puerta. Cuando la puerta se abre, cantan: —Somos María y José, buscando posada. Al principio la familia no los deja entrar; entonces los caminantes vuelven a cantar. Por fin dejan entrar a María y José. Luego todos entran y celebran con una fiesta.

Making Tamales

This is a scene from my parents' kitchen. Everybody is making tamales. My grandfather is wearing blue overalls and a blue shirt. I'm right next to him with my sister Margie. We're helping to soak the dried leaves from the corn. My mother is spreading the cornmeal dough on the leaves and my aunt and uncle are spreading meat on the dough. My grandmother is lining up the rolled and folded tamales ready for cooking. In some families just the women make tamales, but in our family everybody helps.

La Tamalada

Ésta es una escena de la cocina de mis padres. Todos están haciendo tamales. Mi abuelo tiene puesto rancheros azules y camisa azul. Yo estoy al lado de él, con mi hermana Margie. Estamos ayudando a remojar las hojas secas del maíz. Mi mamá está esparciendo la masa de maíz sobre las hojas, y mis tíos están esparciendo la carne sobre la masa. Mi abuelita está ordenando los tamales que ya están enrollados, cubiertos y listos para cocer. En algunas familias sólo las mujeres preparan tamales, pero en mi familia todos ayudan.

171

Watermelon

It's a hot summer evening. The whole family's on the front porch. My grandfather had brought us some watermelons that afternoon. We put them in the refrigerator and let them chill down. After supper we went out to the front porch. My father cut the watermelon and gave each one of us a slice.

It was fun to sit out there. The light was so bright on the porch that you couldn't see beyond the edge of the lit area. It was like being in our own little world.

Sandía

Es una noche calurosa de verano. Toda la familia está en el corredor. Mi abuelo nos había traído unas sandías esa tarde. Las pusimos en el refrigerador para enfriarlas. Después de la cena, salimos al corredor. Mi padre cortó la sandía y nos dio un pedazo a cada uno.

Era divertido estar sentados allá afuera. La luz del corredor era tan fuerte que no se podía ver más allá del área que estaba iluminada. Era como estar en nuestro propio pequeño mundo.

The Virgin of San Juan

A mother and son have gone to church and she's doing some praying. In the meantime, her son starts entertaining himself by taking things out of her purse. She lets him for awhile. Then he hands her a handkerchief. I don't know if he thought that maybe she was crying and needed her handkerchief, or whether he was just playing with it and she took it away from him.

La Virgen de San Juan

Una madre y su hijo han ido a la iglesia y ella está rezando. Mientras tanto, el hijo se entretiene sacando cosas de su cartera. Ella se lo permite por un rato. Luego él le entrega un pañuelo. No sé si es que el niño pensó que su madre estaba llorando y necesitaba su pañuelo, o si el niño estaba jugando con el pañuelo y su madre se lo quitó.

Healer

This is a scene at a neighbor's house. The lady in bed was very sick with the flu. She had already been to a regular doctor and had gotten prescription drugs for her chest cold. But she had also asked a healer, a curandera, to do a final cleansing or healing for this flu. So the curandera came over and did a cleansing using branches from the rue tree. She also burned copal incense in a coffee can at the foot of the bed. Curanderas know a lot about healing. They are very highly respected.

Curandera

Ésta es una escena en la casa de una vecina. La mujer que está en cama estaba muy enferma con influenza. Ya había visto a un doctor y había conseguido una receta médica para sus pulmones. Pero también le había pedido a una curandera que le hiciera una limpieza final o cura para su enfermedad. Así que la curandera vino e hizo una limpieza usando ramas de ruda. También quemó incienso de copal en una lata de café al pie de la cama. Las curanderas saben mucho y ayudan mucho a la gente. Por eso se las respeta tanto.

Beds for Dreaming

My sister and I used to go up on the roof on summer nights and just stay there and talk about the stars and the constellations. We also talked about the future. I knew since I was 13 years old that I wanted to be an artist. And all those things that I dreamed of doing as an artist, I'm finally doing now. My mother was the one who inspired me to be an artist. She made up our beds to sleep in and have regular dreams, but she also laid out the bed for our dreams of the future.

Camas para soñar

Mi hermana y yo solíamos subirnos al techo en las noches de verano y nos quedábamos allí platicando sobre las estrellas y las constelaciones. También platicábamos del futuro. Yo sabía desde que tenía trece años que quería ser artista. Y todas las cosas que soñaba hacer como artista, por fin las estoy haciendo ahora. Mi madre fue la que me inspiró a ser artista. Ella nos tendía las camas para que durmiéramos y tuviéramos sueños normales, pero también preparó la cuna para nuestros sueños del futuro.

All in the Family

Write a Journal Entry

Kingsville, Texas, Here I Come!

If you could visit Carmen Lomas Garza's family, what would you like to do with them? Where would you go? Which foods would you try? Write a journal entry about your visit.

Draw a Picture

Family Album

Do you remember a special day spent with your family? Draw a picture of that day. When you finish, share your picture with your family.

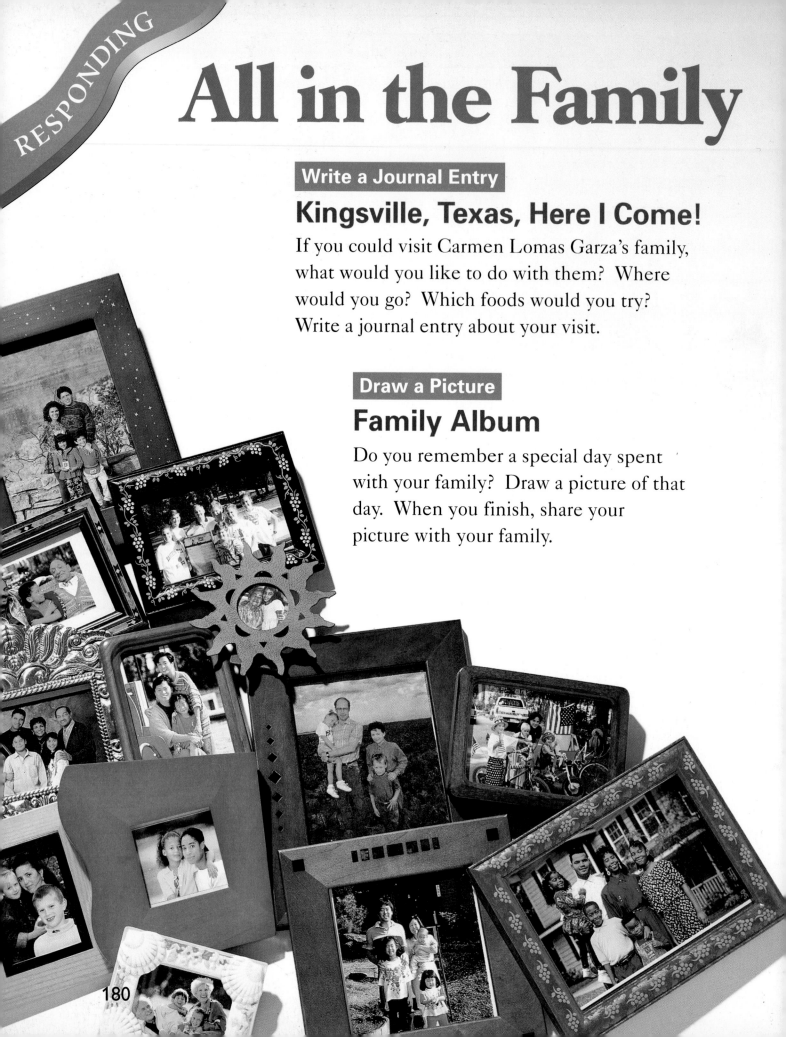

Away from Town

Away from the street lights,
away from town,
stars are more shiny
and hang more down.

Out in the country
where spaces grow,
stars are more many
and hang more low.

Aileen Fisher

181

City

Langston Hughes

In the morning the city
Spreads its wings
Making a song
In stone that sings.

In the evening the city
Goes to bed
Hanging lights
About its head.

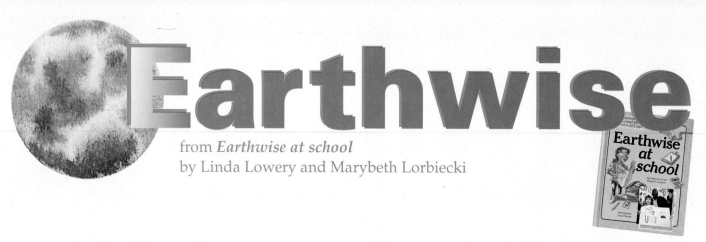

Earthwise

from *Earthwise at school*
by Linda Lowery and Marybeth Lorbiecki

What Does Earthwise Mean?

Have you heard about the bad things happening to the earth — oil spills, garbage piles, air pollution, poisoned rivers, and things like that? Don't let them get you down. There are things each one of us can do to make the planet healthier. And we can do them wherever we are — in our apartments or houses, our classrooms or schoolyards, our neighborhood parks or county woods.

First we need to find out as much information as we can about how the earth works. Then we will be able to take actions that make sense for the whole planet — actions that are earthwise.

184

Cloudy Skies

Since cities are so full of people, factories, and traffic, city air is usually more polluted than country air.

On some days, people in large cities, such as Los Angeles and Mexico City, are told to stay indoors as much as possible. The air outside is too dirty to breathe.

What is your city or town like? Count the smokestacks near you. Ask the factory owners what chemicals they put into the air and what they are doing to stop polluting.

Stand on a street corner, and count the cars that go by. How many people does each car carry? Could these people get around town in a different way? Ask people in your neighborhood what they think can be done. Are they doing anything? Are you?

Air Test

How can you test the air you breathe every day?

1 Spread a thin layer of petroleum jelly on the inside of two wide-mouth glass jars.

2 Place one jar on a shelf in your classroom. Place the other jar in a safe location outside.

After one week, compare the jars. Which jar is darker? What do you think caused this? If either of the jars shows a lot of pollution, what are you going to do? It's probably time to do more research. Call your national, state, or city pollution-control agency and ask them to do an official test of the air near and in your school.

Fewer Cars = Cleaner Air

Even if we could clean up all the smoke from factories, the air would still not be clean. Why not?

Because the exhaust from cars, trucks, and planes is one of the greatest causes of air pollution. So what can you do about that? Plenty!

Walk, skateboard, bike, in-line skate, or roller-skate to places. Share car rides. Take buses, subways, and trains.

Make it a game with your friends and family to see how little you can use a car. Keep track of your miles. Try to go one or two miles less by car each week.

City Solutions

- If every two or more persons in the U.S. going to school or work rode together, we would save more than 600,000 gallons of gasoline every day. Think of how much less air pollution there would be!

- In Boulder, Colorado, there are Bike-to-Work days. Prizes are awarded to the companies with the most employees riding bikes to work.

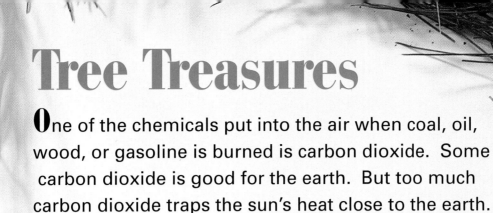

Tree Treasures

One of the chemicals put into the air when coal, oil, wood, or gasoline is burned is carbon dioxide. Some carbon dioxide is good for the earth. But too much carbon dioxide traps the sun's heat close to the earth. Then our climate becomes too hot.

This overwarming is called the greenhouse effect. Fortunately, there is a way to clean the air and fight the greenhouse effect — plant trees. Trees absorb carbon dioxide, and they make shade. Every tree you plant makes the earth cleaner and cooler.

How to Plant a Tree

1. Get permission from the owner of the land.
2. Keep the roots moist and handle them gently.
3. Pick a spot that gets some sun each day.
4. Dig a hole twice as big as the roots.
5. Hold the tree in the hole, and gently cover the roots with dirt. Pack the dirt down gently to remove any air pockets.
6. Water thoroughly right away and then once every day for the first week. Afterward water once a week, if you can.

Meet the Author

Belinda Rochelle grew up hearing stories about the great boxer Joe Louis from her grandparents. They used to listen to his fights on the radio, back in the days when few people owned televisions and boxing wasn't televised. *When Jo Louis Won the Title* is a story about those days.

Meet the Illustrator

Larry Johnson knew he wanted to be an artist ever since he was in the third grade. In addition to illustrating sports books such as *The Jesse Owens Story*, Johnson works as a sports cartoonist for the *Boston Globe* and has his own publishing company.

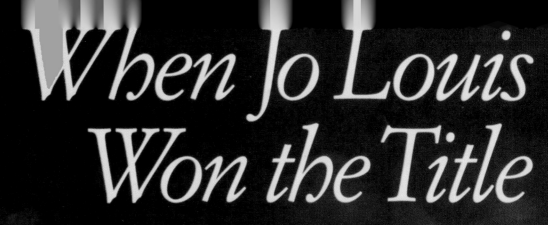

When Jo Louis Won the Title

Belinda Rochelle   Illustrated by Larry Johnson

JO LOUIS sat perched on the top step of ten steps, waiting for her grandfather, John Henry.

"Is that my favorite girl in the whole wide world?" he said as he strolled up the street. He leaned over and picked up Jo Louis, swung her round and round until her ponytails whirled like the propellers of a plane, swung her round and round until they were both dizzy with gasps, swung her round and round until they were both dizzy with giggles.

John Henry's brown eyes twinkled as he returned Jo Louis to the top step and sat down next to her. The smile quickly disappeared from Jo Louis's face. "Why such a sad face on a pretty girl?" he asked.

Tomorrow was a special day for Jo Louis. The first day at a new school. "I don't want to go to school!" Jo Louis said to her grandfather. "I don't want to be the new girl in a new neighborhood at a new school."

John Henry put his arm around her and pulled her close. "Why don't you want to go to school?" he asked.

"I'll probably be the shortest kid in class, or I'll be the one who can't run as fast as the other kids. I finish every race last."

"It's just a matter of time before a new school is an old school. Just a matter of time before you'll be able to run really fast, and you won't always finish last," he said, patting her hand. "What's the real reason you don't want to go to school?" John Henry asked.

Jo Louis shook her head. It was hard to explain. She just knew it would happen. Someone would ask THE question. IT was THE question, the same question each and every time she met someone new: *"What's your name?"*

It was that moment, that question, that made Jo Louis want to disappear. And it really wouldn't make a difference if she were taller, and it wouldn't make a difference that she was the new kid in school, and it wouldn't make a difference if she could run really fast. She just wished that she didn't have to tell anyone her name.

Her grandfather picked her up and placed her on his knee. "Let me tell you a story," he said.

"When I was just a young boy living in Mississippi," he began, "I used to dream about moving north. To me it was the promised land. I wanted to find a good job in the big city. Cities like Chicago, St. Louis.

"But everybody, I mean everybody, talked about Harlem in New York City. Going north, it was all anybody ever talked about. I would sit on the front porch and just daydream about those big-city places. The way some folks told it everything was perfect. Even the streets in the big city were paved with gold, and it was all there just waiting for me."

John Henry's eyes sparkled as his voice quickened. "When I saved enough money, I crowded onto the train with other small-town folks headed north. Everything I owned fit into a torn, tattered suitcase and a brown box wrapped in string.

"I rode the train all day and all night. Like a snake winding its way across the Mississippi River, that train moved slowly through farmlands and flatland, over mountains and valleys, until it reached its final destination."

Jo Louis closed her eyes. She loved her grandfather's stories — his words were like wings and other things. She listened closely until she felt she was right there with him.

197

"'New York City! New York! New York!'
the conductor bellowed as the train pulled into
the station.

"I headed straight to Harlem. I had never seen buildings so tall. They almost seemed to touch the sky. Even the moon looked different in the big city. The moonlight was bright and shining, the stars skipped across the sky. The streets sparkled in the night sky's light. It was true! The streets did seem to be paved in gold!

"I walked up and down city streets that stretched wide and long. I walked past a fancy nightclub, where you could hear the moaning of a saxophone and a woman singing so sad, so soft, and so slow that the music made me long for home.

"And then, all of a sudden the sad music changed to happy music. That saxophone and singing started to swing. Hundreds of people spilled out into the sidewalks, waving flags, scarves, waving handkerchiefs and tablecloths. Hundreds of people filled the streets with noise and laughter, waving hats and anything and everything, filling the sky with bright colors of red, white, green, yellow, blue, purple, and orange.

"Everybody was clapping, hands were raised high to the sky. Up and down the street, people were shouting and singing. Cars were beeping their horns; bells were ringing.

"'Excuse me.' I patted a woman on the shoulder. 'What's going on?' I asked.

"The woman smiled. She was pretty with soft, brown hair and a friendly smile. 'Why, haven't you heard?' she said. 'Joe Louis won the title fight. My name is Mary' — she held out her hand — 'and your name is . . . ?'"

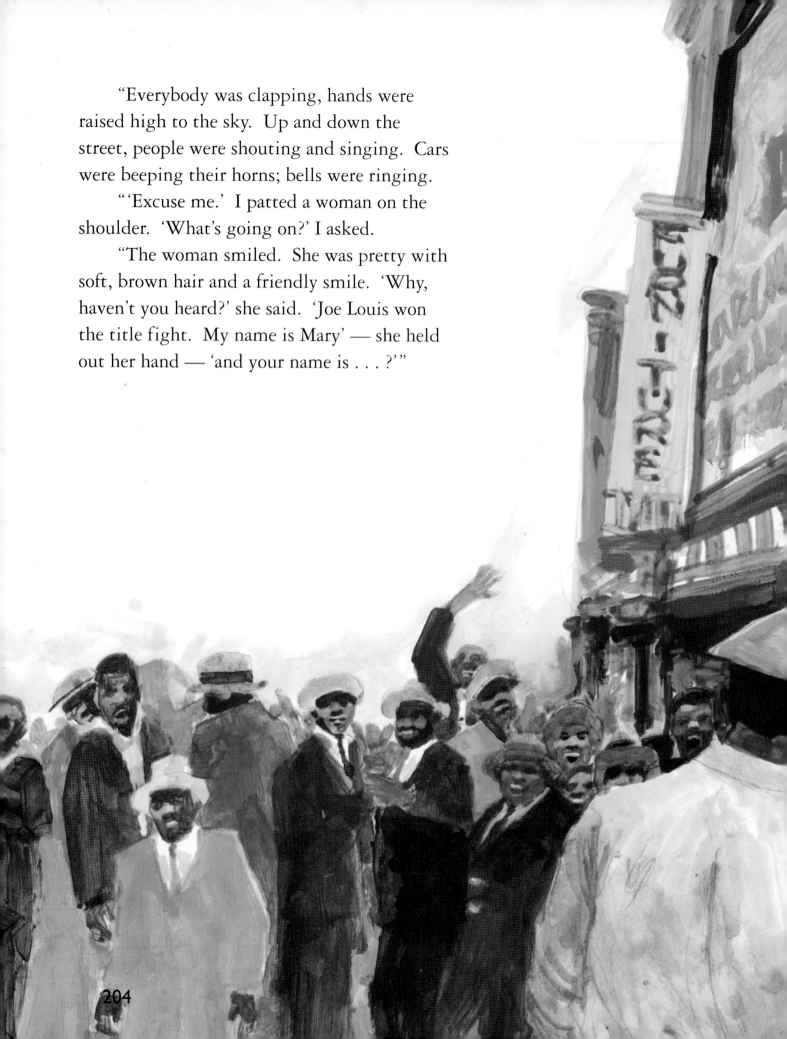

205

John Henry smiled and hugged Jo Louis close. "It was a special night for me. It was a special night for black people everywhere. Joe Louis was the greatest boxer in the world. He was a hero.

"That night he won the fight of his life. A fight that a lot of people thought he would lose. Some folks said he was too slow, others said he wasn't strong enough. But he worked hard and won. It was a special night, my first night in the big city, and Joe Louis won the fight. But the night was special for another reason."

"It was the night you met Grandma," Jo Louis said, and she started to smile.

"It was a special night that I'll never forget. I named your father Joe Louis, and he named you, his first child, Jo Louis, too." Her grandfather tickled her nose. "That was the night you won the title. You should be very proud of your name. Every name has a special story."

The next day Jo Louis took a deep breath as she walked into her new school classroom and slipped into a seat.

The boy sitting next to Jo Louis tapped her on the shoulder. "My name is Lester. What's your name?"

Jo answered slowly, "My name is Jo . . . Jo Louis." She balled her fist and closed her eyes and braced herself. She waited, waited for the laughter, waited for the jokes. She peeked out of one eye, then she peeked out the other eye.

209

"Wow, what a great name!" he said, and smiled.

Name Your Choice

Make a Mural

Let's Celebrate!

Jo Louis's grandfather told her about a celebration that he remembered. Think about a special event that happened in your community. Who was there? What did you do? With your classmates, make a mural showing the event.

Share a Personal Story

A Great Name

There's an interesting story about how Jo Louis got her name. Is there a story behind *your* name? Maybe you were named after a relative, or perhaps you have a nickname. Tell your classmates the story. If you don't know a story about your name, make one up.

The Pool Somersault
A True Story by Joyce Hsieh

When something happened to Joyce at her neighbor's pool, she decided to write about it.

The Pool Somersault

Splash! I went into the water headfirst and did a somersault! That's a day I'll never forget!

It was a hot, hot day. Was I glad when my neighbors said I could go in their pool! When I asked my mother if I could go, she said yes, but I had to take my sister with me.

When I got there, I ran to the slide. When I got on, it was slippery. I accidentally slid down headfirst,

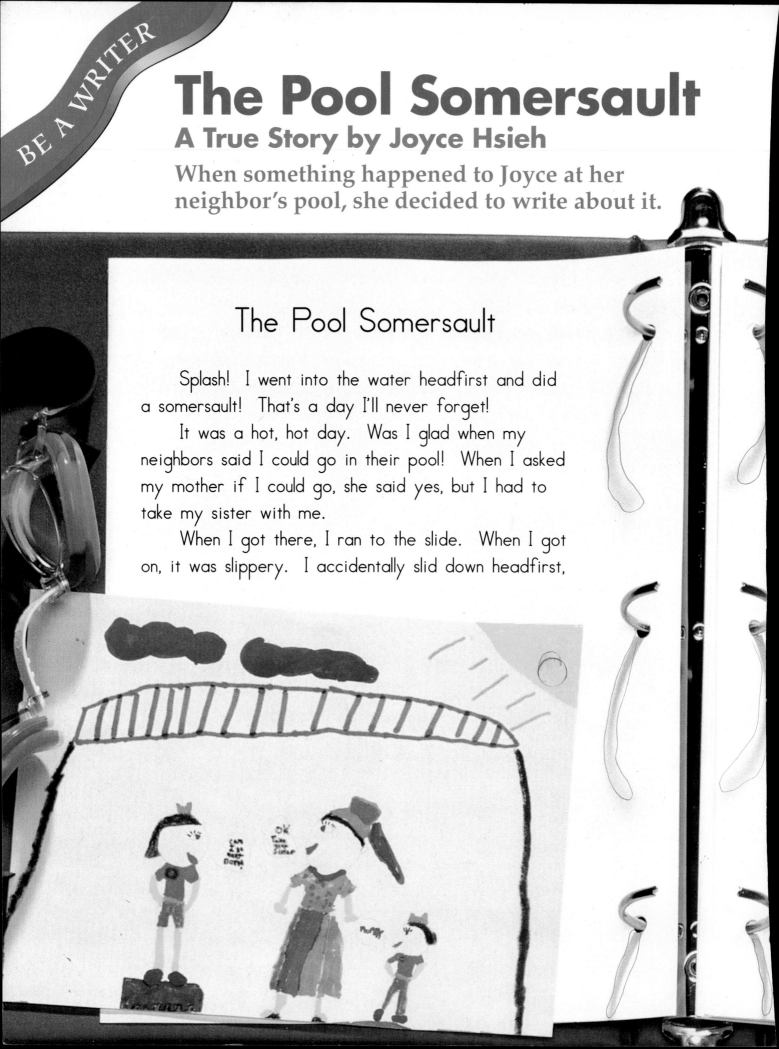

and the rest of my body went into the water in a somersault! I could not believe it! It was the first time that I ever did a somersault in the water. When I went into the water, it was exciting and scary all at the same time. It gave me a good feeling after it was over because I'd never done a somersault in the water before, but I landed so badly. My leg was bleeding and even had a little hole in it. It hurt, but I didn't cry or anything. My neighbor's baby, Chuckie, and my sister were staring at me, and they laughed at me. Both tried to copy me, but I stopped them. I was worried that they would fall down and break something.

When I got home, I told my mom what happened. She seemed surprised but glad that I didn't hurt myself too badly. What an exciting day that was!

Joyce Hsieh
Paloma Elementary School
San Marcos, California

Joyce likes to write about animals, places she has been, and her family. She also likes to write letters to friends. She chose to write about the pool somersault because it was fun and interesting. Playing games, tennis, and the piano are some things that Joyce enjoys doing. When she grows up, Joyce wants to be an artist.

Painting the Town

oil paint

turpentine

linseed oil

Coming to the Celebration
Mattie Lou O'Kelley, 20th century
oil paint

palette knife

oil brushes

The Builders
Jacob Lawrence, 1974
silk screen print

silk screen
printing ink

silk screen

ink

squeegee

Shawnee Indians Having Cornbread Dance

Earnest Spybuck, c. 1910
watercolor

sketch
pencil

watercolor
paper

watercolor
paint

watercolor
paint

mixing
palette

May Day, Central Park

Maurice Prendergast, 1901
watercolor

watercolor
brushes

water jar

Some of the words in this book may have pronunciations or meanings you do not know. This glossary can help you by telling you how to pronounce those words and by telling you the meanings for the words as they are used in this book.

You can find out how to pronounce any glossary word by using the special spelling after the word and the key that runs across the bottom of the glossary pages.

The full pronunciation key on the next page shows how to pronounce each consonant and vowel in a special spelling. The pronunciation key at the bottom of the glossary pages is a shortened form of the full key.

Full Pronunciation Key

Consonant Sounds

b	**b**i**b**, ca**bb**age	kw	**ch**oir, **qu**ick	t	**t**igh**t**, stopp**ed**
ch	**ch**ur**ch**, sti**tch**	l	**l**id, need**l**e, ta**ll**	th	ba**th**, **th**in
d	**d**ee**d**, mail**ed**, pu**dd**le	m	a**m**, **m**an, du**mb**	*th*	ba**th**e, **th**is
f	**f**ast, **f**i**f**e, o**ff**, **ph**rase, rou**gh**	n	**n**o, sudd**en**	v	ca**v**e, val**v**e, **v**ine
g	**g**a**g**, **g**et, fin**g**er	ng	thi**ng**, i**nk**	w	**w**ith, **w**olf
h	**h**at, **wh**o	p	**p**o**p**, ha**pp**y	y	**y**es, **y**olk, on**i**on
hw	**wh**ich, **wh**ere	r	**r**oar, **rh**yme	z	ro**s**e, si**z**e, **x**ylophone, **z**ebra
j	**j**u**dg**e, **g**em	s	mi**ss**, **s**auce, **sc**ene, **s**ee	zh	gara**g**e, plea**s**ure, vi**s**ion
k	**c**at, **k**i**ck**, s**ch**ool	sh	di**sh**, **sh**ip, **s**ugar, ti**ss**ue		

Vowel Sounds

ă	r**a**t, l**au**gh	ŏ	h**o**rrible, p**o**t	ŭ	c**u**t, fl**oo**d, r**ou**gh, s**o**me
ā	**a**pe, **ai**d, p**ay**	ō	g**o**, r**ow**, t**oe**, th**ough**	û	c**i**rcle, f**u**r, h**ea**rd, t**er**m, t**ur**n, **u**rge, w**or**d
â	**ai**r, c**a**re, w**ea**r	ô	**a**ll, c**au**ght, f**o**r, p**aw**	yo͞o	c**u**re
ä	f**a**ther, k**o**ala, y**a**rd	oi	b**oy**, n**oi**se, **oi**l	yo͝o	ab**u**se, **u**se
ĕ	p**e**t, pl**ea**sure, **a**ny	ou	c**ow**, **ou**t	ə	**a**bout, sil**e**nt, penc**i**l, lem**o**n, circ**u**s
ē	b**e**, b**ee**, **ea**sy, p**ia**no	o͝o	f**u**ll, t**oo**k, w**o**lf		
ĭ	**i**f, p**i**t, b**u**sy	o͞o	b**oo**t, fr**ui**t, fl**ew**		
ī	b**y**, p**ie**, h**igh**				
î	d**ea**r, d**ee**r, f**ie**rce, m**e**re				

Stress Marks

Primary Stress ′: bi•ol•o•gy [bī **ŏl′** ə jē]
Secondary Stress ′: bi•o•log•i•cal [bī′ ə **lŏj′** i kəl]

Pronunciation key © 1993 by Houghton Mifflin Company. Adapted and reprinted by permission from *The American Heritage Children's Dictionary*.

A

ac•cent (**ăk´** sĕnt´) *noun* A small detail that looks different than the things around it, usually added for color or decoration: *The bedroom was blue with pink pillows for* **accent**.

art•ist (**är´** tĭst) *noun* **1.** A person who practices an art, such as painting or music: *The* **artist** *displayed her paintings in the town hall.* **2.** A person who shows great skill in what he or she does: *Mr. Brown's bake shop has the prettiest wedding cakes in town. He is a true* **artist**.

B

bel•low (**bĕl´** ō) *verb* To say in a deep, loud voice: *The police officer* **bellowed** *to the crowd to get away from the burning building.*

brace (brās) *verb* To get ready for something difficult or unpleasant: *As Eric walked toward the lake, he* **braced** *himself against the shock of the cold water.*

C

cus•tom (**kŭs´** təm) *noun* Something that members of a group usually do: *One birthday* **custom** *is to blow out the candles on a birthday cake.*

D

de•sign (dĭ **zīn´**) *noun* A pleasing pattern of lines and shapes: *The wrapping paper was decorated with colorful flower and leaf* **designs**.

di•a•mond (**dī´** ə mənd) *noun* A shape (◊) with four equal sides.

I

in•spire (ĭn **spīr´**) *verb* To cause someone to think or act in a particular way: *My grandmother, who made all of her own clothes,* **inspired** *me to learn to sew.*

M

mar•ket (**mär´** kĭt) *noun* A place where people buy and sell goods: *Mr. Choy goes to the* **market** *each*

ă rat / ā pay / â care / ä father / ĕ pet / ē be / ĭ pit / ī pie / î fierce / ŏ pot / ō go / ô paw, for / oi oil / o͞o took

Glossary 3

morning to buy fresh fish for his restaurant.

market

 P

pyr•a•mid (**pĭr´** ə mĭd) *noun* A figure that has a flat bottom and sides shaped like triangles.

R

rec•og•nize (**rĕk´** əg nīz´) *verb* To see and know from past experience: *Even from far away, Becky could **recognize** her brother in the crowd by his red cowboy hat.*

 S

scene (sēn) *noun* A view of a place: *The photograph showed a **scene** of a cabin by a lake.*

 **T**

tat•tered (**tăt´** ərd) *adjective* Torn and ragged looking: *By the time Andy got the stuffed animal away from the puppy, it was torn and **tattered**.*

TATTERED

Tattered comes from the Scandinavian word *tötturr*, which means "rag."

---

ti•tle (**tīt´** l) *noun* A name given to a person to show rank, office, or job: *After finishing medical school, my uncle's new **title** became Doctor.*

ti•tle fight (**tīt´** l fīt) *noun* A boxing match to determine the champion: *Joe Louis first won the heavyweight championship in a **title fight** in 1937.*

tri•an•gle (**trī´** ăng´ gəl) A shape (△) with three sides.

 **W**

whirl (wûrl) *verb* To spin around in circles: *The children **whirled** round and round until they felt dizzy.*

ōō boot / ou out / ŭ cut / û fur / hw which / th thin / *th* this / zh vision / ə about, silent, pencil, lemon, circus

Glossary 4

ACKNOWLEDGMENTS

For each of the selections listed below, grateful acknowledgment is made for permission to excerpt and/or reprint original or copyrighted material as follows:

Selections

Selection from *Earthwise at school,* by Linda Lowery and Marybeth Lorbiecki. Copyright © 1993 by Linda Lowery and Marybeth Lorbiecki. Reprinted by permission of Carolrhoda Books.

Family Pictures, written and illustrated by Carmen Lomas Garza. Copyright © 1990 by Carmen Lomas Garza. Reprinted by permission of Children's Books Press.

A Fruit & Vegetable Man, by Roni Schotter, illustrated by Jeanette Winter. Text copyright © 1993 by Roni Schotter. Illustrations copyright © 1993 by Jeanette Winter. Reprinted by permission of Little, Brown and Company.

When Jo Louis Won the Title, by Belinda Rochelle, illustrated by Larry Johnson. Text copyright © 1994 by Belinda Rochelle. Illustrations copyright © 1994 by Larry Johnson. Reprinted by permission of Houghton Mifflin Company. All rights reserved.

Poetry

"Away from Town," from *Runny Days, Sunny Days,* by Aileen Fisher. Copyright © 1958 by Aileen Fisher. Reprinted by permission of the author.

"City," by Langston Hughes, from *The Langston Hughes Reader.* Copyright © 1958 by Langston Hughes. Copyright renewed 1986 by George Houston Bass. Reprinted by permission of Harold Ober Associates Inc.

Additional Acknowledgments

Special thanks to the following teacher whose student's composition is included in the Be a Writer feature in this theme: Linda Chick, Paloma Elementary School, San Marcos, California.

CREDITS

Illustration 127–144 Jeanette Winter **151–179** Carmen Lomas Garza **181, 184** Pam Rossi **189–210** Larry Johnson

Assignment Photography Cover/Back cover Tracey Wheeler (background) **Title page** Tony Scarpetta (background, bl inset); Tracey Wheeler (tr inset) **120–121** Tracey Wheeler **122–123, 124–125, 126–127** Tony Scarpetta **145** Tracey Wheeler **150–151** Glenn Kremer **180, 184–185** Tony Scarpetta **185** Tracey Wheeler (insets) **186–187** Tony Scarpetta **188** Katherine Lambert **211** Tracey Wheeler **212–213** Tony Scarpetta **214–215, 216–217** Banta Digital Group **Back cover insets** Tracey Wheeler (tm); Tony Scarpetta (m, bm); Banta Digital Group (bl)

Photography 126 Courtesy of Roni Schotter (tl); Courtesy of Jeanette Winter (br) **146–149** Fred Boyles **182, 183** © Ken Briggs/© Tony Stone Images/Chicago, Inc. **213** Courtesy of Joyce Hsieh **214** Little, Brown & Co. **215** Francine Seders Gallery LTD **216** National Museum of the American Indian **217** The Cleveland Museum of Art **Glossary 4** M. Dwyer/Stock Boston (tl)